Looking at Countries
IRAN

Kathleen Pohl

FRANKLIN WATTS
LONDON • SYDNEY

512304

This edition first published in 2008 by Franklin Watts

Franklin Watts
338 Euston Road
London NW1 3BH

First published in 2008 by Gareth Stevens Publishing
1 Reader's Digest Road
Pleasantville
NY 10570-7000 USA

Dewey number: 915.5
ISBN: 978 0 7496 8244 6

Senior Managing Editor: Lisa M. Guidone
Senior Editor: Barbara Bakowski
Creative Director: Lisa Donovan
Designer: Tammy West
Photo Researcher: Sylvia Ohlrich
Reading Consultant: Susan Nations, M.Ed.

Photo credits: (t=top, b=bottom, l=left, r=right)
Cover (main) SuperStock; Cover (inset) Franco Origlia/Getty Images; title page
SuperStock; p. 4 Hermann Dornhege/VISUM/The Image Works; p. 6. Vodjani/Ullstein/Peter
Arnold; p. 7t Rob Howard/Corbis; p. 7b Tor Eigeland/Alamy; p. 8 EmmePi Images/Alamy; p.
9t Morteza Nikoubazl/Reuters/Landov; p. 9b M. Phillip Kahl/Photo Researchers; p. 10 Stefan
Noebel-Heise/Transit/Peter Arnold; p. 11t Silke Reents/VISUM/The Image Works;
p. 11b Mohammad Kheirkhah/UPI/Landov; p. 12l Raheb Homavandi/Reuters/Landov;
p. 12r Majid/Getty Images; p. 13 Earl Kowall/Corbis; p. 14 Caren Firouz/Reuters/Landov;
p. 15t Franco Pizzochero/Marka/Age Fotostock; p. 15b Michelle Falzone/Age Fotostock;
p. 16 Bernd Weissbrod/DPA/Landov; p. 17t Enric Marti/AP Images; p. 17b Vodjani/Ullstein/
Peter Arnold; p. 18 Patrick Snyder/Lonely Planet Images; p. 19t Sergio Pitamitz/Marka/
age fotostock; p. 19b SuperStock; p. 20t Gulfimages/Getty Images; p. 20b JTB Photo
Communications/Alamy; p. 21t TH Foto/StockFood; p. 21b Morteza Nikoubazl/Reuters/
Landov; p. 22 Dana Wilson/Peter Arnold; p. 23t Carl Purcell/Corbis; p. 23b SuperStock;
p. 24 Serge Sibert/Cosmos/Aurora Photos; p. 25t Xinhua/Landov; p. 25b Shehzad Noorani/
Majority World/The Image Works; p. 26 SuperStock; p. 27 SDBReligion/Alamy (2). Every
attempt has been made to clear copyright. Should there be any inadvertent omission
please apply to the publisher for rectification.

Printed in China

Franklin Watts is a division of Hachette Children's Books, an Hachette Livre UK company.
www.hachettelivre.co.uk

Contents

Where is Iran?

Iran is in south-western Asia, in an area known as the Middle East. Iran shares borders with seven other countries. These are Iraq, Turkey, Pakistan, Afghanistan, Armenia, Azerbaijan and Turkmenistan.

Did you know?

Iran is one of the oldest countries in the world. It was once called Persia. People have lived there for almost 5,000 years.

Atlantic Ocean

ASIA

EUROPE

IRAN

MIDDLE EAST

AFRICA

Indian Ocean

Iran is part of the Middle East.

The Azadi Tower in Tehran was built in 1971 and is a symbol of Iran. Some people call it the Freedom Tower.

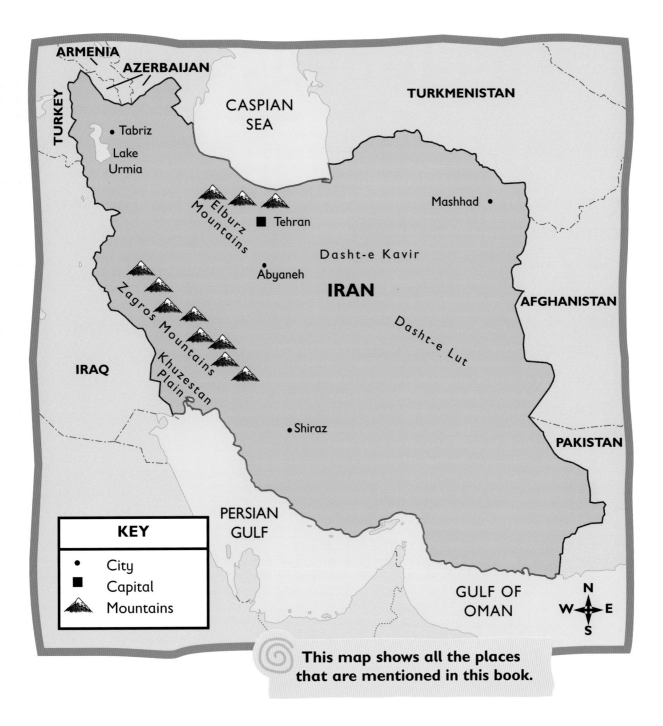

ARMENIA

AZERBAIJAN

TURKMENISTAN

TURKEY

CASPIAN
SEA

• Tabriz

Lake
Urmia

Elburz
Mountains

■ Tehran

Mashhad •

Dasht-e Kavir

• Abyaneh

IRAN

Zagros Mountains

AFGHANISTAN

Dasht-e Lut

IRAQ

Khuzestan
Plain

PAKISTAN

• Shiraz

PERSIAN
GULF

KEY

• City
■ Capital
🏔 Mountains

GULF OF
OMAN

N
W ✦ E
S

**This map shows all the places
that are mentioned in this book.**

Tehran is the capital of Iran and is also the country's
largest city. Tehran has modern skyscrapers as well
as extremely old buildings and places of prayer,
called mosques. Offices, schools, banks and parks line
the streets of Tehran.

The landscape

Mountains and deserts make up most of Iran. The two main mountain ranges are the Elburz and the Zagros. Earthquakes in these mountains sometimes make the ground shake. This can destroy cities, damage homes and cause many deaths. Major earthquakes are rare but small ones happen almost daily.

Did you know?

Since 1991, earthquakes in Iran have killed more than 18,000 people and injured 53,000 people.

The snowcapped Elburz Mountains are in the northern part of Iran.

A high, dry plateau, or flat area of land, makes up the centre of Iran. Few people live in this huge desert area. The Dasht-e Kavir, or Great Salt Desert, has a salty crust. Sand dunes make up the Dasht-e Lut desert.

Most people live in the lowlands in the north near the sea. The land and climate there are good for farming.

Iran's oil fields are in the Khuzestan Plain, along the Persian Gulf.

Weather and seasons

Most of Iran is very dry, with few lakes or freshwater streams. Most rivers and lakes dry up in the hot summer. The greatest rainfall is in the north near the Caspian Sea and very little rain falls in the rest of the country. The rainiest season is winter, from November through to March.

Did you know?

For thousands of years, people in Iran have used a water supply system called a *qanat* (or *kanat*). It collects underground water and moves it through tunnels to places where people need it.

Qanats, like this one, help Iranian people by moving water to places where they need it.

People enjoy
skiing in the
Elburz Mountains
in winter.

Lake Urmia is a salt lake.
It is one of the few lakes in
Iran that does not dry up
in the heat of summer.

Summers are coolest in the mountains. In the
south, along the Persian Gulf, summers are hot
and damp. Strong winds blow hot, dry air from
the west across central Iran during the summer.

Winters in the mountains can be very cold and
can bring plenty of snow and ice. Spring and
autumn are mostly mild.

Iranian people

About 65 million people live in Iran. Almost all of them are Muslims, people who follow Islam.

The government of Iran is based on the rules of Islam. These tell people how to dress and behave. For instance, men and women must sit apart on a bus or a train. They stand in separate queues in shops. Beaches and ski slopes have different areas for men and women.

In public, girls and women must cover their hair and wear clothes that cover the body. They are only allowed to show the face, toes and hands.

Did you know?

In the holy month of Ramadan, adult Muslims do not eat or drink between sunrise and sunset.

There are women-only carriages on underground trains.

Women only

A crowd of Muslims gathers in front of a mosque to pray.

All Muslims must pray at five different times each day. Friday is the Islamic holy day of the week. Offices and schools are closed.

School and family

Children must go to primary school for five years, from the age of six. Boys and girls go to separate schools. They study maths, science, Islam and they learn Persian, the language of Iran. At the end of primary school, all students take a test. Those who pass can attend a three-year middle school.

Some students then go to a four-year trade school or an academic high school. Students who want to go to university must take a national exam. Iran has more than 30 free universities.

In Iran, children go to primary school for five years.

A young boy studies the Koran with his teacher.

An Iranian family share a meal together. The food is served on a cloth spread over a carpet.

Did you know?

Students study the Koran, the holy book of Islam, more than any other book in school.

Most families are large. Grandparents often live with their children and grandchildren. The father is the head of the household while the mother usually cooks, cleans and cares for the children. In the countryside, women help with farm work. In the cities, some women work outside the home.

Country

One in three people in Iran lives in the countryside. Most of them are farmers. Some use modern tractors to farm, while others use mules. Farmers grow wheat, barley, rice and nuts. Figs, dates, melons, olives and spices are other farm produce. Near the Caspian Sea, many people are fishermen.

Did you know?

Some people like to eat fish eggs, called caviar. They come from a type of large fish called a sturgeon that lives in the Caspian Sea.

Many farmers grow fruit or nuts. This man is harvesting dates from a date palm tree.

Fishermen at work in the Caspian Sea.

The village of Abyaneh is one of the oldest in Iran. It is known for its red soil and clay buildings.

Some villages in Iran do not have electric power for light or running water. People get clean at the public baths in the village.

Some people who live in the country are nomads. They move from place to place to graze their goats and sheep.

City

Most people in Iran live and work in cities. About 12 million people live in Tehran, the capital and Iran's largest city. More than half of them were born somewhere else, though. The city is home to Iran's main airport and largest university.

Did you know?

For thousands of years, traders travelled along the Silk Road through Iran. Some of Iran's big cities are along this route.

Tehran's streets are crowded with cars, buses and taxis.

Mashhad is a large city and a major trade centre in the east of the country. Tabriz, in the north-west, is famous for its bazaar. This is a large market where people buy and sell food and goods. Weavers make and sell fine rugs at the bazaar in Tabriz.

Many cities blend the old with the new. In the old parts of towns are mosques, market places and ancient buildings. The new areas have big shops, modern blocks of flats and wide streets.

People shop at large bazaars, like this one in Tehran. They buy food, handmade rugs and other crafts.

Many visitors come to this garden in the old city of Shiraz.

Iranian homes

Most homes in the country are square houses made of sun-dried mud bricks. The houses have only one or two rooms. A single room may be used as a bedroom, a dining room and a sitting room at different times of the day. Most houses have no windows and are topped by flat roofs. At the centre of most villages is a mosque.

Did you know?

Most homes in Iran do not have tables and chairs. People sit on cushions on the floor to eat their meals.

This man is making the mud bricks that will be used to build houses.

These nomads have set up their tent at the foot of the Zagros Mountains.

Many people live in modern flats in big cities, such as Tehran.

Iranian nomads live in tents, which they take with them when they travel. The tents are made of animal skins or goat hair.

In the cities, many people live in modern blocks of flats. Most are made of brick or cement.

Food

People in Iran eat bread with most meals. They serve rice with vegetables or cover it with a thick sauce. Dolmas are popular. They are vine leaves, stuffed with rice and meat. Iranians eat lamb, beef and fish but not pork, as it is forbidden by Islam. Fruit, such as melons and dates, and nuts are favourite foods, too.

Dolmas are vine leaves stuffed with mince and rice.

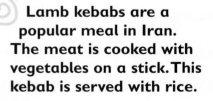

Lamb kebabs are a popular meal in Iran. The meat is cooked with vegetables on a stick. This kebab is served with rice.

Did you know?

Chai is the word for 'tea' in Iran.

This seller serves tea and snacks at a city bazaar.

Teenagers everywhere like to eat at fast-food restaurants!

Many people enjoy eating at restaurants. They go to tea houses to drink tea and meet friends. A drink made with yogurt, or sour milk, is popular, too.

At work

Some people in Iran work in banks, schools and offices. Others are doctors and nurses in hospitals.

In the Persian Gulf area, many people work in the oil business. About 100 wells are drilled in Iran each year. Oil is one of the main products Iran sells to other countries. Other important goods are fruit, nuts, spices, fish eggs (caviar) and rugs.

Iran is known for its silk cloth. Silk thread is made by caterpillars called silkworms. Farmers in north-western Iran raise silkworms for their silk.

Huge ships carry oil out of the Persian Gulf.

Weavers dry their handmade rugs in the sun.

Did you know?

Iran is known all over the world for its beautiful rugs.

Workers in Shiraz, in southern Iran, make fine metal bowls and vases.

People work in factories, too. They make bricks, cement, cloth and leather goods. In ports on the coasts, people load ships with goods to be sent to other countries.

Having fun

Nowruz is the New Year holiday in Iran. It starts on the first day of spring and lasts for 13 days. Shops and schools are closed. Families visit each other, eat sweets and nuts and give gifts. On the thirteenth day, people meet for a picnic. They also enjoy music and dancing.

Did you know?

Football is very popular in Iran. Fans crowd into Azadi Stadium in Tehran to watch the national team play matches.

Families observe Nowruz (the New Year holiday) with a picnic. It is bad luck to stay inside on the last day of this 13-day-long celebration.

Playing and watching sport are popular activities. Favourite sports include football, basketball, volleyball, wrestling and polo. People also like to walk and ski in the mountains.

Many people in Iran enjoy listening to the radio, watching television and going to films. Chess is a popular game to play with friends.

A young football fan cheers at a match.

Children play on a village playground.

Iran: the facts

- Iran is an Islamic republic. The country's official name is the Islamic Republic of Iran. It is ruled by religious leaders.

- Iran has a president, who is elected by the people.

- Iran is divided into 30 regions. Each has its own capital city and government.

- Men and women in Iran who are at least 15 years old may vote in the country's elections.

- Persian, or Farsi, is the language of Iran.

The flag of Iran has three bars – green, white and red. The Arabic words 'God is great' are written along the edges of the green and red bars. The national symbol is in the middle of the white bar.

CENTRAL BANK OF THE
ISLAMIC REPUBLIC OF IRAN

50000

FIFTY THOUSAND RIALS

The Iranian
unit of money
is the rial.

Did you know?

When creating rugs,
weavers often make a
mistake – on purpose!
They want to show
their belief that only
God is perfect.

People in Iran have woven
beautiful rugs for 2,500 years.

Glossary

Bazaar an outdoor marketplace where food and other goods are bought and sold.

Dolmas a dish of vegetables or vine leaves stuffed with herbs, rice or meat.

Factories buildings where workers make goods.

Graze to put animals out to eat grass in fields.

Islam the religion of Muslims.

Kebabs cubes of meat cooked with vegetables on a stick.

Koran (also spelled Qur'an) the holy book of Islam.

Middle East an area of southwest Asia and northern Africa stretching from the eastern Mediterranean to Iran.

Mosques Islamic houses of prayer.

Muslims people who follow the teachings of the Prophet Muhammad, the founder of Islam.

Nomads people who don't live in one place but wander from place to place to find food or graze their animals.

Persia the ancient name of modern-day Iran.

Persian the modern language of Iran; also known as Farsi.

Plateau a high, flat area of land.

Polo a game similar to hockey but played on horseback using long-handled mallets and a wooden ball.

Qanat an underground system of tunnels to transport water.

Ramadan a holy month of fasting observed by adult Muslims, when they do not eat or drink during daylight hours.

Republic a kind of government in which decisions are made by the people of the country and their representatives.

Rial unit of currency, or money, in Iran.

Silk Road an ancient trade route that crossed Asia from China to the Mediterranean.

Vine leaf the leaf of the grape plant.

Find out more

http://news.bbc.co.uk/cbbcnews/hi/guides/default.stm
Click on the guide about Islam to learn more about the national religion of Iran.

www.thebritishmuseum.ac.uk/forgottenempire/index.html
This site, set up by the British Museum, explores the history of ancient Persia, the kingdom that ruled the lands that are now modern Iran.

Some Persian words

Persian is spoken by about 40 million people in Iran. It is written using a different alphabet from our own.

Speak some Persian:

English	Say...
yes	baleh
no	nah
please	loftan
excuse me	be bakh shid
thank you	mamnoon am
What is this?	In chi-ye?
Greetings/Hello!	Salam!
Goodbye	Khoda hafez
God willing.	Enshallah.

Here are a few Persian words that have become part of the English language:
aubergine bazaar lemon azure caviar

My map of Iran

Trace this map and colour it in and use the map
on page 5 to write the names of all the towns.

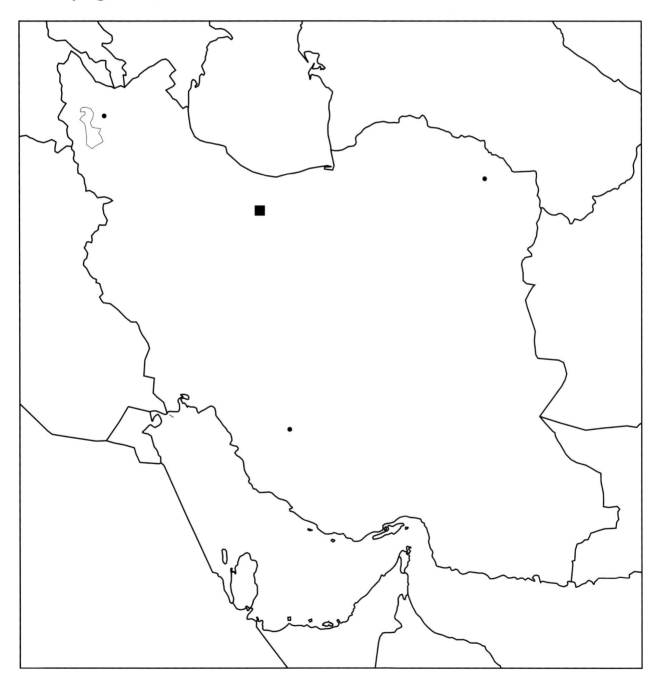

PERTH AND KINROSS LIBRARIES

Index